WHAT IS WONDER?

WHAT is WONDER?

A Timeless Workbook to Get to Know Yourself Better

Kayvan Kian

TO THE MOON PUBLISHING
New York, New York

WHAT IS WONDER?
A Timeless Workbook to Get to Know Yourself Better

ISBN 978-90-833864-2-3 *Hardcover*
978-90-833864-4-7 *Paperback*
978-90-833864-3-0 *Ebook*

TO THE MOON PUBLISHING
New York, New York

Author photograph by Giovanni Siani
Cover and layout design by John van der Woude, JVDW Designs

ΓΝΩΘΙ ΣΑΥΤΟΝ

—Inscription, Temple of Apollo at Delphi

Dedicated to the
Unnoticed Treasures of Life

WELCOME

Knowing yourself more fully can lead to better leadership, relationships, and decision-making. You can also pursue it for its own sake.

However, we don't often get the chance to turn our attention inward, to notice aspects of ourselves that go unnoticed in a world full of demands, information overload, and distractions.

So why wait? Feel free to seize the opportunity, and immerse yourself in this workbook full of timeless questions with room for reflection.

With awareness, playfulness, and courage, the following questions can help you explore your inner life further to get to know yourself better.

Bonam Fortunam!

Reflections, Memories & Ideas

How well do you know yourself?

How have you developed your self-knowledge over time?

Reflections, Memories & Ideas

How well do you want to know yourself?

Why?

Reflections, Memories & Ideas

What adventures do you still hope to experience in life?

What makes them so appealing?

Reflections, Memories & Ideas

When was the last time you surprised yourself?

What made it so surprising?

Reflections, Memories & Ideas

Who are the closest people in your life?

What needs do they most fulfill for you?

Reflections, Memories & Ideas

What is the sweetest dream you've ever had?

What could have been its meaning?

Reflections, Memories & Ideas

What is most important to you in life?

How have your views on this developed over time?

Reflections, Memories & Ideas

What is something you do differently from others around you?

What has this brought you?

Reflections, Memories & Ideas

Where do you get your ideas from?

Where else would you like to get your ideas from?

Reflections, Memories & Ideas

What makes you feel at home?

Where have you felt this?

Reflections, Memories & Ideas

Growing up, who did you always want to become?

Why?

Reflections, Memories & Ideas

What are your goals in the short term?

Where did these goals come from?

Reflections, Memories & Ideas

Which book has had the most impact on you?

In what ways?

Reflections, Memories & Ideas

What does nature mean to you?

How have your views on this developed over time?

Reflections, Memories & Ideas

Who do you admire?

What would you like to learn from them?

Reflections, Memories & Ideas

If you could write a song today, what would it be about?

What would be the first lines of the song?

Reflections, Memories & Ideas

When have you felt most lucky in life?

What was its impact on you?

Reflections, Memories & Ideas

When was the last time you felt nostalgic about something?

What were you missing most?

Reflections, Memories & Ideas

Is there anything you regret doing?

Is there anything you regret not doing?

Reflections, Memories & Ideas

What are the most important events
for you in the coming year?

What feelings do they bring up for you?

Reflections, Memories & Ideas

How do you currently deal with conflict?

How has this changed over time?

Reflections, Memories & Ideas

Which sports do you enjoy the most?

What about it do you enjoy so much?

Reflections, Memories & Ideas

Which secrets would you want to keep with you forever?

Which secrets would you want to share over time?

Reflections, Memories & Ideas

Which movie could you watch over and over again?

What makes it so appealing?

Reflections, Memories & Ideas

What is missing in your life these days?

How are you dealing with this?

Reflections, Memories & Ideas

In which areas do you feel supported in life?

Are there other areas you would like
to experience support?

Reflections, Memories & Ideas

If you could give yourself a gift, what would it be?

Why?

Reflections, Memories & Ideas

Which skills are you good at?

Which of these give you energy?

Reflections, Memories & Ideas

Which skills are you not so good at (yet)?

Which of these, however, still give you energy?

Reflections, Memories & Ideas

What is worth fighting for in life?

Why is that so precious to you?

Reflections, Memories & Ideas

Looking back at the past few months,
what are you most grateful for?

Why?

Reflections, Memories & Ideas

What is your first childhood memory?

How has this influenced your life so far?

Reflections, Memories & Ideas

What is the quote you would like to be remembered by?

Why?

Reflections, Memories & Ideas

What makes you laugh?

What could this say about you?

Reflections, Memories & Ideas

What is worth celebrating in your life?

What could a next celebration look like?

Reflections, Memories & Ideas

What do you hope to get out of this workbook?

How is that going so far?

Reflections, Memories & Ideas

What re-energizes you?

How are these things a part of your life?

Reflections, Memories & Ideas

What de-energizes you?

What about these things is most de-energizing?

Reflections, Memories & Ideas

What do you regret regretting?

Why?

Reflections, Memories & Ideas

What is your favorite time of year?

How come?

Reflections, Memories & Ideas

Where are you too hard on yourself?

Where are you too soft on yourself?

Reflections, Memories & Ideas

What is something that used to scare you but no longer does?

What role did you play in this?

Reflections, Memories & Ideas

What changes would you like to make in your life?

How come?

Reflections, Memories & Ideas

What kind of environment brings out the best in you?

What makes it so?

Reflections, Memories & Ideas

What do you have faith in?

What role does this faith play in your life?

Reflections, Memories & Ideas

What knowledge would you like to acquire?

What makes this so interesting to you?

Reflections, Memories & Ideas

How are you feeling today?

How come?

Reflections, Memories & Ideas

What question would you most like to be asked?

How would you answer that question?

Reflections, Memories & Ideas

What principles have guided your life?

What have they brought you?

Reflections, Memories & Ideas

How do you feel about the passage of time in your life?

What could you learn from these feelings?

Reflections, Memories & Ideas

How good are you at saying no
to the things you don't want?

How do you feel about this?

Reflections, Memories & Ideas

What does family mean to you?

In what ways has this changed over time?

Reflections, Memories & Ideas

What has been on your mind most these days?

How come?

Reflections, Memories & Ideas

What would your ideal week look like?

What about this would be fulfilling to you?

Reflections, Memories & Ideas

What is something you wish
you could do one more time?

Why?

Reflections, Memories & Ideas

What are the biggest distractions in your life?

What are they distracting you from?

Reflections, Memories & Ideas

Which childhood dreams have you already fulfilled?

How does that make you feel?

Reflections, Memories & Ideas

In what ways could these days,
in the future, become the "good old days"?

What more comes to mind?

Reflections, Memories & Ideas

Which recent dreams can you still remember?

What meaning could they have?

Reflections, Memories & Ideas

When was the last time you made a significant mistake?

How did you deal with this?

Reflections, Memories & Ideas

Looking back on your life, which moments evoke a sense of self-compassion?

What would you tell your younger self in those moments if you had the chance?

Reflections, Memories & Ideas

What do you like to do for fun?

Which of these do you enjoy the most?

Reflections, Memories & Ideas

What have you not seen that you still hope to see one day?

Why?

Reflections, Memories & Ideas

What would it take for you to feel successful in the future?

Where does this definition of success come from?

Reflections, Memories & Ideas

Which patterns do you notice most in your relationships?

Where do these patterns come from?

Reflections, Memories & Ideas

What risks are worth taking in life?

Why?

Reflections, Memories & Ideas

What could be something you are running away from?

Since when?

Reflections, Memories & Ideas

Which parts of your life might you be putting on hold?

How come?

Reflections, Memories & Ideas

What is your first response under pressure?

What is your second response?

Reflections, Memories & Ideas

What do you think others appreciate about you?

What do you appreciate about yourself?

Reflections, Memories & Ideas

What kind of items do you like to have in your surroundings?

What do they bring you?

Reflections, Memories & Ideas

What does friendship mean to you?

How is this different compared to the past?

Reflections, Memories & Ideas

Which place would you still like to visit one day?

What makes this place so appealing?

Reflections, Memories & Ideas

How do the different aspects of
your life relate to each other?

How would you like the different aspects
of your life to relate to each other?

Reflections, Memories & Ideas

Which values are so essential to you that it hurts when they're breached?

How do you typically respond when they're breached?

Reflections, Memories & Ideas

What needs have you not yet fulfilled?

What got in the way?

Reflections, Memories & Ideas

Who had the most positive impact on you growing up?

What part of that are you most grateful for?

Reflections, Memories & Ideas

What are things you consider to be
most within your control these days?

What are things you consider to be
least within your control these days?

Reflections, Memories & Ideas

What makes you feel awe?

How has this developed over the years?

Reflections, Memories & Ideas

What art would you like to learn?

What could this bring you?

Reflections, Memories & Ideas

Who do you miss?

What do you miss most about them?

Reflections, Memories & Ideas

Which childhood story captured your imagination the most?

What effect might this have had on you?

Reflections, Memories & Ideas

Where do you feel the safest?

How come?

Reflections, Memories & Ideas

What is your favorite music?

What makes this music so special to you?

Reflections, Memories & Ideas

Who brings out the best in you?

How does this person do that?

Reflections, Memories & Ideas

When times are hard,
what gives you the courage to go on?

How has this developed over the years?

Reflections, Memories & Ideas

What do you have in abundance?

What would you like to have in abundance?

Reflections, Memories & Ideas

What are you most looking forward to in the coming year?

What makes this so appealing?

Reflections, Memories & Ideas

Which real-life or fictional person would you like to meet?

What would you like to ask them?

Reflections, Memories & Ideas

What do you feel most
responsible for in your personal life?

What do you feel most responsible for in the world?

Reflections, Memories & Ideas

What would you like to give to others?

Why?

Reflections, Memories & Ideas

Which risks are you trying to avoid?

What worries you most about these?

Reflections, Memories & Ideas

How has kindness played a role in your life?

What effect has this had on you?

Reflections, Memories & Ideas

Which opportunities would you like to notice better?

What would excite you most about these?

Reflections, Memories & Ideas

What would you do if you had a year off?

What would these activities bring you?

Reflections, Memories & Ideas

What does money mean to you right now?

How would you like this meaning to change over time?

Reflections, Memories & Ideas

What makes your heart sing?

How come?

Reflections, Memories & Ideas

What is something you've been curious about lately?

What makes this so interesting to you?

Reflections, Memories & Ideas

What would you do differently if
you knew no one would judge you?

How would you judge yourself in that scenario?

Reflections, Memories & Ideas

If your life were to be made into a movie,
what would it be called?

What makes this title so fitting?

Reflections, Memories & Ideas

What would you start if you knew you couldn't fail?

What would this bring you?

Reflections, Memories & Ideas

What message would you like
to give to future generations?

How has your thinking on this topic
developed over the years?

Reflections, Memories & Ideas

Which skills would you like to become exceptionally good at?

What makes mastering these skills so appealing to you?

Reflections, Memories & Ideas

If you could do it all over again,
what would you do more of?

What got in your way?

Reflections, Memories & Ideas

What would you teach if you had
the chance to have your own class?

What makes this subject so interesting to you?

Reflections, Memories & Ideas

Which year would you travel to
in the past if you had a time machine?

What would you hope to experience then?

Reflections, Memories & Ideas

What are you holding on to that
no longer really serves you?

What is making it difficult for you to let go?

Reflections, Memories & Ideas

What is something you have no doubts about?

How does this truth affect the decisions in your life?

Reflections, Memories & Ideas

Which patterns have you noticed in your thinking over the years?

How do these help or hinder you?

Reflections, Memories & Ideas

What are the thoughts and feelings
this workbook is bringing up for you so far?

What more comes to mind?

Reflections, Memories & Ideas

Have you ever changed an
undesirable situation you were in?

If so, how did you do that?

Reflections, Memories & Ideas

When do you feel most impatient?

What do you do in those situations?

Reflections, Memories & Ideas

If you could relive one day, which day would it be?

Can you describe the most special moments of that day?

Reflections, Memories & Ideas

How can someone make you feel loved?

How do you show your love to others?

Reflections, Memories & Ideas

What are your favorite words?

What makes them so special for you?

Reflections, Memories & Ideas

What does it take for you to trust someone?

How have your views on this changed over time?

Reflections, Memories & Ideas

What are words you've never dared to speak?

How come?

Reflections, Memories & Ideas

How would you ideally start your mornings?

What would that bring you?

Reflections, Memories & Ideas

Which clothes best express who you are?

Why?

Reflections, Memories & Ideas

Knowing what you know now, what is one thing you would have done differently in the past?

Knowing what you thought then, what were you hoping for?

Reflections, Memories & Ideas

What is the best compliment you've ever received?

What makes it so memorable for you?

Reflections, Memories & Ideas

What are you deeply proud of?

What makes it so special for you?

Reflections, Memories & Ideas

Which of your strengths can you rely on?

How have these helped you?

Reflections, Memories & Ideas

Who's there for you these days?

Who are you there for?

Reflections, Memories & Ideas

When do you feel most carefree?

What makes it so?

Reflections, Memories & Ideas

What are your most unfulfilled wishes so far?

What are your most fulfilled wishes so far?

Reflections, Memories & Ideas

How might you be getting in your own way at times?

How has this changed over time?

Reflections, Memories & Ideas

What kind of person do you want to be
in the next chapter of your life?

What kind of person do you not want to be
in the next chapter of your life?

Reflections, Memories & Ideas

What do you do when things get too difficult to deal with?

When do they get too difficult?

Reflections, Memories & Ideas

Which activities make you forget about time?

What might these activities have in common?

Reflections, Memories & Ideas

Are there any new boundaries in your life worth setting?

What would these boundaries protect?

Reflections, Memories & Ideas

What would you like to do right now?

If not now, when?

Reflections, Memories & Ideas

Is there something that
people often ask you for advice on?

How did you develop this expertise?

Reflections, Memories & Ideas

How do you want to be remembered?

Why is that important to you?

Reflections, Memories & Ideas

What is something about you that has never changed?

How do you feel about this?

Reflections, Memories & Ideas

Which wounds can still hurt at times?

How do you deal with this?

Reflections, Memories & Ideas

Where is your attention most of the time:
the past, present, or future?

Where would you like your attention to be?

Reflections, Memories & Ideas

What kind of person do you enjoy spending time with?

What makes it so enjoyable?

Reflections, Memories & Ideas

When do you feel most misunderstood?

When do you feel most understood?

Reflections, Memories & Ideas

What are your favorite indoor activities?

What are your favorite outdoor activities?

Reflections, Memories & Ideas

What do you think your future self
would like to tell you today?

What would you like to tell your future self today?

Reflections, Memories & Ideas

What is going well for you?

What role did you play in this?

Reflections, Memories & Ideas

When was the last time you felt inspired?

What were the sources of this inspiration?

Reflections, Memories & Ideas

When did you feel most satisfied in your life?

What made that so?

Reflections, Memories & Ideas

When was the last time you felt courageous?

What might you have learned from this?

Reflections, Memories & Ideas

What would you consider the background music in this chapter of your life?

What other music would you like to play in the background?

Reflections, Memories & Ideas

What is something you have
that money could never buy?

How did this become part of your life?

Reflections, Memories & Ideas

Which childhood memory do you cherish the most?

What feelings does that bring up for you?

Reflections, Memories & Ideas

What does work mean to you?

In what ways has this changed over time?

Reflections, Memories & Ideas

What would you like to dream tonight?

Why?

Reflections, Memories & Ideas

What is one thing you wish to do
that you have never done before?

How would this experience make you feel?

Reflections, Memories & Ideas

How do you define beauty?

What role does this play in your life?

Reflections, Memories & Ideas

Which traditions and rituals do you value?

What feelings do they bring up for you?

Reflections, Memories & Ideas

How aware are you in general of your own emotions?

In what ways do you express these emotions?

Reflections, Memories & Ideas

If you could spend time in the future,
how far ahead would you go, for how long?

What would you hope to experience then?

Reflections, Memories & Ideas

Have you given up on anything?

What feelings does that bring up for you?

Reflections, Memories & Ideas

How are you taking care of yourself?

Which needs are you meeting this way?

Reflections, Memories & Ideas

To what extent do you sense an internal resistance to a goal you've set for yourself?

What could be the root of this resistance?

Reflections, Memories & Ideas

What are you waiting for?

How long are you willing to wait?

Reflections, Memories & Ideas

What are things you can't get enough of?

How much of these things do you already have?

Reflections, Memories & Ideas

When do your actions and words differ from each other?

What could this say about your real preferences?

Reflections, Memories & Ideas

What is something you need to accept but haven't fully done so yet?

What is holding you back?

Reflections, Memories & Ideas

What does it take for you to
change your mind about something?

How is this helping or hindering you?

Reflections, Memories & Ideas

What is your perspective on life?

How has this changed over time?

Reflections, Memories & Ideas

What makes a good society in your view?

What role would you like to play in such a society?

Reflections, Memories & Ideas

What promise to yourself do you still need to fulfill?

What has gotten in the way?

Reflections, Memories & Ideas

What would you never do?

What will this protect you from?

Reflections, Memories & Ideas

What is the most difficult decision you've ever made?

How did you eventually make this decision?

Reflections, Memories & Ideas

What are the most important lessons
you've learned in your life?

How did you learn them?

Reflections, Memories & Ideas

When was the last time you tried something new?

What brought you to do so?

Reflections, Memories & Ideas

What would you consider a good life?

What more comes to mind?

Reflections, Memories & Ideas

Add your own question...

Reflections, Memories & Ideas

Add your own question...

Reflections, Memories & Ideas

Add your own question...

Reflections, Memories & Ideas

Add your own question...

Reflections, Memories & Ideas

Add your own question...

ABOUT THE AUTHOR

Kayvan Kian is an entrepreneur, teacher, and senior advisor to McKinsey & Company in Amsterdam. His work has helped thousands of leaders and teams thrive during difficult times.

As the founder of the Young Leaders Forum, Kayvan has given guest lectures at Harvard Business School, HEC, Sciences Po, and more. His previous books *What Is Water?* and *What Is Wisdom?* became instant bestsellers, and he publishes articles on leadership and decision-making. He holds an MBA from INSEAD in France and a degree in both Economics and Law from the Erasmus University in the Netherlands.

www.kayvankian.com

More by Kayvan Kian

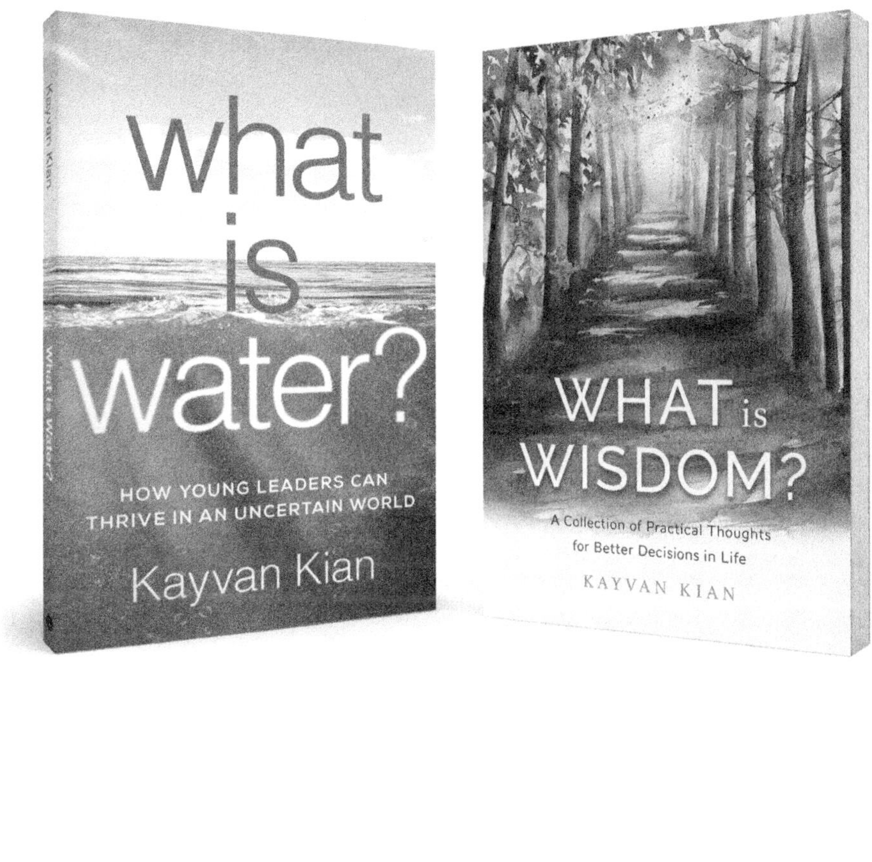

Listen!

Did you hear it?